First Facts®

U.S. Military Forces

THE UNITED STATES ARMY

BY MICHAEL GREEN

CAPSTONE PRESS
a capstone imprint

First Facts are published by Capstone Press,
1710 Roe Crest Drive, North Mankato, Minnesota 56003
www.capstonepub.com

Library of Congress Cataloging-in-Publication Data
Green, Michael, 1952–
    The United States Army / by Michael Green.
    p. cm.—(First facts. U.S. Military Forces.)
    Audience: Grades K-3.
    Summary: "Provides information on the training, missions, and equipment used by the
United States Army"—Provided by publisher.
    Includes bibliographical references and index.
    ISBN 978-1-4765-0069-0 (library binding)
    ISBN 978-1-4765-1585-4 (ebook pdf)
1. United States. Army—Juvenile literature. I. Title.
UA25.G79 2013
355.00973—dc23   2012033247

Editorial Credits

Aaron Sautter, editor; Ashlee Suker, designer; Eric Manske, production specialist

Photo Credits

Corbis: Bettmann, 6; DoD photo by Staff Sgt. Michael L. Casteel, US Army, 5; U.S. Air Force photo by Staff
SGt. Angelita M. Lawrence, 1; U.S. Army photo 9, 12, 15, 18, 21, Sgt. Michael J. MacLeod, 17, cover, Spc.
Derek Del Rosario, 13, Spc. Ryan Hallock, 14; U.S. Navy photo by MC1 Eileen Kelly Fors, 10

Artistic Effects

Shutterstock: Kirsty Pargeter, Redshinestudio, Vilmos Varga

Printed in the United States of America in North Mankato, Minnesota.
092012   006933CGS13

TABLE OF CONTENTS

CHAPTER ONE

FIGHTING FOR FREEDOM

A **squad** of U.S. Army soldiers is on duty in Afghanistan. Suddenly enemy fighters open fire. The U.S. soldiers take cover and shoot back. The **firefight** finally ends when the enemies retreat. The U.S. soldiers have won this fight. But it won't be their last.

squad—a unit of nine to 10 soldiers in the Army

firefight—exchange of weapon fire between two military units

FACT

The U.S. Army was first known as the Continental army. It was led by General George Washington.

The U.S. Army is a key part of the U.S. military. It defends the United States and **democracy** around the world.

The Continental Congress created the U.S. Army on June 14, 1775. The Army has fought in many wars since then. More than 1.3 million U.S. soldiers have fought and died in battle.

CHAPTER TWO

A POWERFUL FORCE

The U.S. Army is one of the largest in the world. It has more than 480,000 active soldiers. They are ready to go on any **mission** at any time. The Army also has 190,000 reserve soldiers. They are often called to serve during national emergencies.

mission—a military task

FACT

Soldiers and officers serve at least one tour of duty. Each tour lasts three to six years.

The U.S. Army is made up of **enlisted** soldiers and officers. Soldiers do most of the fighting in combat. Officers lead troops and make decisions during battles.

Every soldier has a job to do on the battlefield. Soldiers may fire heavy weapons, operate **radar**, or control missile launchers.

enlist—to voluntarily join a branch of the military

radar—a device that uses radio waves to track the location of objects

CHAPTER THREE

BECOMING A SOLDIER

Army **recruits** go to basic training for 10 weeks. They wake up before dawn and train hard all day. They also learn military rules and how to use weapons.

FACT

Basic training includes running many miles each day, climbing walls, and going through obstacle courses.

recruit—a new member of the armed forces

After basic training, soldiers learn skills needed for their Army jobs. Soldiers can choose from more than 150 different Army jobs. These jobs include doctors, lawyers, engineers, and many more.

College graduates can become Army officers at Officer Candidate School. There they learn battle skills needed to be an officer.

Some people attend the U.S. Military Academy at West Point, New York. There **cadets** learn military traditions and leadership skills. They become officers when they graduate.

CHAPTER FOUR

GEARED UP FOR BATTLE

The U.S. Army uses a lot of high-tech gear. Soldiers use night-vision goggles to find enemies in the dark. **Global Positioning System (GPS)** locators help them find enemy locations.

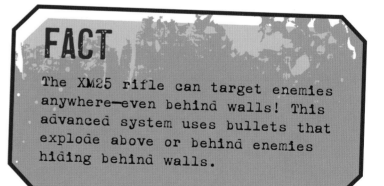

FACT

The XM25 rifle can target enemies anywhere—even behind walls! This advanced system uses bullets that explode above or behind enemies hiding behind walls.

Global Positioning System—a satellite system that determines any position in the world

Soldiers also use powerful
weapons in combat. Assault rifles,
machine guns, and sniper rifles
help soldiers fight the enemy.

FACT

Strykers are fast armored vehicles. They can quickly deliver troops and help fight in battles.

Combat vehicles are key to the Army's success. Abrams tanks provide major firepower. Bradley Fighting Vehicles help support and protect soldiers. Apache attack helicopters are armed with machine guns and missiles. Unmanned Aerial Vehicles (UAVs) help fight enemies in dangerous locations.

CHAPTER FIVE

STANDING SAFE AND STRONG

The U.S. Army works to keep soldiers safe in battle. Unmanned Predator **drones** can quickly strike at enemies from a distance.

The U.S. Army has highly trained soldiers. It uses high-tech weapons and gear. The Army will keep fighting to keep America safe and strong.

drone—an unmanned, remote-controlled aircraft or missile

FACT

The U.S. Army uses several remote-controlled robots. The robots help carry heavy equipment and explore dangerous locations.

GLOSSARY

cadet (kuh-DET)—a military student

democracy (di-MAH-kruh-see)—a kind of government in which the people choose their leaders

drone (DROHN)—an unmanned, remote-controlled aircraft or missile

enlist (in-LIST)—to voluntarily join a branch of the military

firefight (FIRE-fite)—an exchange of weapon fire between two military units

Global Positioning System (GLOH-buhl puh-ZI-shuh-ning SISS-tuhm)—an electronic tool used to find the location of an object; this system is often called GPS

missile (MISS-uhl)—an explosive weapon that can travel long distances

mission (MISH-uhn)—a military task

obstacle course (OB-stuh-kuhl KORSS)—a series of barriers that soldiers must jump over, climb, or crawl through

radar (RAY-dar)—a device that uses radio waves to track the location of objects

recruit (ri-KROOT)—a new member of the armed forces

squad (SKWAHD)—a unit of nine to 10 soldiers in the Army

READ MORE

Besel, Jennifer M. *The Green Berets.* Elite Military Forces. Mankato, Minn.: Capstone Press, 2011.

David, Jack. *United States Army.* Armed Forces. Minneapolis: Bellwether Media, 2008.

Gonzalez, Lissette. *The U.S. Military: Defending the Nation.* Dangerous Jobs. New York: PowerKids Press, 2008.

INTERNET SITES

FactHound offers a safe, fun way to find Internet sites related to this book. All of the sites on FactHound have been researched by our staff.

Here's all you do:

Visit *www.facthound.com*

Type in this code: 9781476500690

Super-cool stuff!

Check out projects, games and lots more at
www.capstonekids.com

INDEX